CW00704375

IMAGES
of America

VAIL
THE FIRST 50 YEARS

Rearing above Vail, the spectacular spires of the Gore Range are a constant reminder of the beauty of the Vail Valley in the Eagle's Nest Wilderness. In both winter and summer, the pinnacles are touched with rosy alpenglow. Whether people are sipping hot chocolate at Mid-Vail on a cold winter day, teeing off on Vail's golf course, or spending an evening at the Vail Amphitheater, the Gore Range has always dominated life at Vail. (Photograph by Shirley Welch.)

On the Cover: In the 1960s, from left to right, Bill Duddy, Susan Rodgers Kurz, Lillian Miller, and Hannes Kurath take a break from skiing to enjoy a glorious spring day on Vail Mountain. (Courtesy of Barry Stott/Stott Shot.)

IMAGES
of America

VAIL
THE FIRST 50 YEARS

Shirley Welch

ARCADIA
PUBLISHING

Copyright © 2012 by Shirley Welch
ISBN 978-1-5316-6443-5

Published by Arcadia Publishing
Charleston, South Carolina

Library of Congress Control Number: 2012942165

For all general information, please contact Arcadia Publishing:
Telephone 843-853-2070
Fax 843-853-0044
E-mail sales@arcadiapublishing.com
For customer service and orders:
Toll-Free 1-888-313-2665

Visit us on the Internet at www.arcadiapublishing.com

Dedicated to all the visitors who have enjoyed the Vail Valley.

CONTENTS

ACKNOWLEDGMENTS

Susie Tjossem, executive director of the Colorado Ski & Snowboard Museum, asked me to compile photographs for an Arcadia book to celebrate Vail's 50th birthday. The Colorado Ski & Snowboard Museum was created to honor Coloradoans who have contributed significantly to the sport of skiing and snowboarding in Colorado. I was honored to work with Susie and the museum to produce this book.

Many people are responsible for gathering these photographs. Albums in attics were dusted, slides were found, and corporations granted permission to use photographs. I would like to thank Betty Josey, Sepp Cheny, Don Johnson, Bob Warner, Bob Ruder, Jebbie Brown, Mauri Nottingham, Tom Steinberg, Robin Litt, the Vail Police Department, the Vail Tennis Center, and Susie Tjossem for finding photographs for me. A thank-you goes to Barry Stott for allowing me to choose photographs from his collection. Jaci Sphuler at the Eagle County Library district scanned the photographs from the historical collection. Loran Moran at the Colorado Ski Museum should be credited for her excellent job of editing the book. Also, I would like to thank Kristin Williams at Vail Resorts for her help. I would like to especially thank both Diana Donovan and Sandy Hinmon for their friendship, photographs, and many stories. Finally, I would like to thank my husband, Don, who brought me to Vail for one year of skiing. One year turned into a lifetime.

Unless otherwise noted, all photographs are courtesy of the Colorado Ski & Snowboard Museum and Shirley Welch.

INTRODUCTION

Eons ago, after the Rocky Mountains finished uplifting and the oceans retreated, gentle mountains formed between the jagged Gore and Sawatch Ranges in central Colorado. Moisture poured in from the west and, blocked by the mountains, dumped hundreds of inches of snow each winter.

Nomadic Ute Indians wandered the area, hunting and moving with the seasons as the deep snows pushed them to lower elevations in the winter. In the 1850s and 1860s, drought besieged the area. Lightning struck the bowls on the south-facing side of the mountains, and fires raged, burning entire hillsides. Over the next 75 years, heavy snowfalls returned, and the remains of the burned forest decayed, leaving mountain slopes devoid of trees. These open bowls remained invisible from the Gore Creek Valley.

Hunters found their way into the valley in the mid-1800s, the most infamous gentleman being Lord Gore, who had arrived from Ireland. Lord Gore spent three years tramping the American West, shooting anything that moved. With dozens of servants, 100 horses, 20 yokes of oxen, and tons of provisions loaded in wagons, Gore meandered through this area. After exhausting his provisions, Gore found himself cornered by a war party of Sioux Indians who stripped him of horses, supplies, and clothes. Eventually, friendly Indians gave him shelter, and he quietly returned to Ireland. By the time Lord Gore left the region, gold and silver had been discovered in the Leadville area. When the Ute Indians were removed, more settlers found the area to their liking. However, the winters were severe, and not many settlers stayed.

When World War II loomed on the horizon, the US Army decided there was a need to train elite mountain troops for winter warfare. The army built a new facility in Eagle Park, a swampy, beaver-populated valley with a railroad stop called Pando. The camp was established there because of its natural setting—a flat valley bottom surrounded by steep hillsides, which was suitable for training in skiing, rock climbing, and cold-weather survival skills. Camp Hale was constructed in 1942, and when in full operation it housed 15,000 soldiers, many of whom were mountaineers, skiers, and ski racers from around the country. Because residents could provide provisions to the soldiers, the Army camp was a boost to incomes in the Gore Creek Valley.

After World War II came to a close, 10th Mountain Division soldier Pete Seibert returned to Colorado to ski race and work at various ski areas. He became friends with Earl Eaton, who had been raised not far from the Gore Valley and hiked and hunted throughout the area. The two men shared a dream—to find and build the best ski area in the world.

Both men ended up working at Loveland Ski Area. One night, while gathered around the potbellied stove at Buckley's Store in Silver Plume, Earl told Pete about the open bowls behind No-Name Mountain. Pete suggested that the two of them take a look. In March 1957, the men strapped on skis with skins and made a seven-hour trek to the top of No-Name Mountain. When they reached the summit, Pete looked right and left at treeless slopes, and he knew they had found their mountain.

They called Earl the "finder" and Pete the "founder." Pete knew people and had connections, and Earl could build things. Together with Bob Fowler, a Denver attorney, and John Conway, a real estate man, Pete and Earl had their team. They formed the Transmontane Rod and Gun Club, pretending to be purchasing the land along Gore Creek for hunting and fishing pleasure. After finding the money to purchase the Hanson Ranch at the base of No-Name Mountain, George Calkins and Jack Tweedy joined the group. The men chose the name *Vail* for the ski mountain. To make it official, the Vail Corporation was formed in 1959 and recruited investors. In 1960, the first board of directors met, which included Fritz Benedict, Dick Hausermen, Jack Tweedy, George Caulkins, Fitzhugh Scott, Peter Seibert, Harley Highboy, Bob Fowler, and Gerry Hart.

The directors wasted little time in making Vail a reality. A town plan was formulated and architectural controls put in place. In the spring of 1962, construction began on the mountain and in the village. Despite setbacks, Vail Mountain opened on December 15, 1962, with a lackluster amount of snow. Lift tickets cost $5.

From the beginning, Vail grew by leaps and bounds. Ownership of the company changed several times. Despite these changes, Vail continued to grow through the decades. In 1989, Vail hosted the World Alpine Championships, and in 2000, Blue Sky Basin opened more ski terrain. Throughout all of the growing pains, its residents have defined Vail's character. Those who came were a little more resilient, a bit more adventurous, and a lot more memorable. The early ones were called pioneers, but anyone who settles in Vail now is equally adventurous. In the future, these "Vailites" will continue to carve Vail's history.

One

BEFORE VAIL

Hundreds of years ago, hunter-gatherers roamed the Rocky Mountains, including the Vail Valley. During the 1800s, fur trading and trapping began in western Colorado. John C. Fremont led an expedition west in the 1840s, crossed Tennessee Pass, and found the Colorado River. Still, the Vail Valley remained undiscovered. A decade later, Lord Gore hunted the area with guide Jim Bridger. For the next several decades, prospectors stalked the area, but still the Vail Valley remained free of white settlers. When the Ute Indians were forcibly removed from Colorado, the population of miners and homesteaders exploded. By 1880, Leadville boasted a population of 40,000. Hunters ventured farther afield to feed the townsfolk, wandering into the Gore Creek valley. When the Denver & Rio Grande Railroad line was built through Leadville, the little valley that had remained hidden was ripe for settlers.

One of the first settlers along Gore Creek was John Wesley Philips and his young wife, Mary, who made their home here in 1884. Mary produced 14 children. John supplied the mining towns with everything from lamb to wild game to potatoes. John built skis out of barn wood, with leather bindings nailed to the slabs. After the bottoms were oiled with goose grease, the boys skied from the top of Vail pass to the ranch. By the early 1900s, other families had joined the Philipses. At the east end of the valley was the Mann Ranch, and along the western end of the valley was the Ruder family's ranch. The Katsos and Kiahitpes families became sheep ranchers. The Kiahitpeses's summer home is now a bus stop in East Vail. Frank and Marge Haas bought 520 acres at the mouth of Red Sandstone Creek from the Kellog family, who had a sawmill on the property. The Haas family sold their ranch at the bottom of No-Name Mountain to the Hanson family.

The traditional east-west route through the Rocky Mountains was over Shrine Pass, which brought travelers to Red Cliff, Gilman, and mining camps in the Homestake Valley. Only a pack trail crossed Black Gore Pass. In 1939, the Colorado State Highway Department decided to build a new road through the area sometimes known as Low Divide, and it picked Charles "Charlie" Vail as the chief engineer for the project. (Courtesy of Vail Resorts.)

Although Vail favored a shorter route over Red Buffalo Pass, that path would have crossed lands in protected primitive areas and was in the direct line for numerous snowslides. Thus, the Black Gore Pass route was chosen. With the summit at 10,617 feet, the new pass was officially named after Charlie Vail, who was called an engineering genius.

10

Considered a marvel of engineering when it was first built, Highway 6 followed the contour of Gore Creek. This 1965 photograph shows the view east of Booth Creek and the north side of the mountain above where the Mountain School campus is today. There are a few homes built in the area. The Kiahitpes ranch house, with the white chimney, is visible. (Courtesy of Sandy Hinmon.)

In the area of East Vail where Big Horn Creek meets Gore Creek, Charles "Porky" Baldauf built the Baldauf ranch home in 1906. Charles and his family farmed lettuce on the 500-acre ranch. The family kept a trained bear, which entertained travelers along Highway 6. The home still stands near its original location on the campus of Vail Mountain School.

Graduation is a time for smiles and photographs. In this 1912 photograph, Edna Baldauf, daughter of Charlie Baldauf, has graduated from Eagle County High School. The school's first class graduated in 1910. Edna later married Carl Norgaard, the son of one of the earliest settlers in Gypsum. She is in the middle, and to the left is a Mr. Heath, principal of Eagle Valley High School. (Courtesy of Eagle County Historical Society.)

Because of the severe winters along Gore Creek, sheep ranching was more profitable than raising cattle. Greek sheepmen Kiahitpes and Katsos purchased the Baldaulf ranch in the 1930s. Gus Kiahitpes built this cabin where Pitkin Creek meets Gore Creek. His brand, the Circle K, was painted high on the white chimney. Today, the building still stands and is a bus stop in East Vail.

Summertime brings out the best along the Gore Creek Valley. It marks a time for recreation, a time for neighbors to get together, and a time for picnics. In this 1930s-era photograph, the Kiahitpes family hosts a barbecue of roasted lamb at their property in East Vail. Sheep were easier to raise in the mountains because they could be tended without much care and could easily be moved down the mountain in the fall, loaded onto freight cars, and taken to Utah for winter grazing. In the photograph are, from left to right, Pete Katsos (in front), Ted Katsos, Gus Kiahtipes, and Frank Haas. Haas owned the ranch that the Hansons purchased, which is now the heart of Vail Village. (Eagle County Historical Society.)

In the beginning, Katstos and Kiahtipes were partners. After the partnership ended, each had his own ranch and grazed sheep on Vail Mountain during the summertime. Many of Vail's early residents on Forest and Rockledge Roads would wake to find sheep surrounding their homes. This 1962 photograph was taken about where Ford Park is today.

Along Gore Creek, where the Ford Amphitheater and Alpine Gardens are today, Henry Anholtz owned 160 acres. A cantankerous man, Henry first tried his hand at mining near the current Vail Public Works facility but failed. Henry's wife lived in this house, which now houses the Vail Nature Center. Henry lived across the creek.

This photograph shows the original root cellar built by Henry Anholtz. It is located east of the footbridge over Gore Creek leading to Ford Park. Potatoes and lettuce could be stored for most of the year after ice was harvested and packed with the vegetables. An antisocial man, Henry threatened trespassers with a rifle. In 1962, he traded some of his land to Vail Associates.

This 1967 photograph shows the Gore Creek schoolhouse. It was a one-room, pitched-roof schoolhouse. It stood on the north side of Gore Creek in West Vail where Safeway is now. Built by parents in 1922 on land donated by Richard Elliott, the Gore Creek schoolhouse was in District 11 and closed as a schoolhouse in 1938. (Courtesy of Sandy Hinmon.)

From 1938 until about 1962, the schoolhouse was used for sheepherders. The Macleod family from Arvada bought the schoolhouse around 1962, and in 1972, they sold the land and donated the schoolhouse to the Town of Vail. It was moved to Ford Park in the 1980s. Today, it serves as a museum and still houses the original blackboard.

In 1887, Jacob and Mary Ruder came to the Gore Creek Valley and homesteaded 160 acres where Intermountain is today. This photograph is of their third home, built around 1915, which they constructed with some additions. The Ruders farmed lettuce. Fortunately, the family held onto the property until the 1960s, when it was sold to a developer.

Not far from the Ruder ranch, Pauline and Henry Elliott built a cabin in 1912 on their 160-acre homestead, located a few doors down from the present-day Savoy Inn. The Elliotts' homestead encompassed land that is now Matterhorn and parts of northwest Vail. The family logged, raised lettuce, and ran a dairy that supplied Camp Hale with milk.

Seen here in 1954, Leonard Ruder, son of Jacob and Mary Ruder, practices moving rocks at the sawmill on Sandstone Creek. Leonard was in charge of building and clearing Gitalong, the one road leading to Mid-Vail, in the spring of 1962. He also cleared Gold Peak, Pickeroon, and Avanti. Ruder's Run is named for Leonard. (Courtesy of Bob Ruder.)

17

In the 1930s, Frank and Margie Haas bought their 520-acre ranch where Sandstone Creek meets Gore Creek. Their house was below the Fleming sawmill. The property was west of Albert Betz's ranch and extended on both sides of Gore Creek from the Anholz property almost to West Vail. In this photograph, Margie and Frank Harnagle bottle-feed spring lambs. (Courtesy of Eagle County Historical Society.)

Ranching at the Sandstone Creek Ranch was an ongoing operation. In the fall, hay was cut and stored in the barn. This photograph from the 1940s shows, from left to right, Jim Fanning, Frank Haas, Cliff Ingram, an unidentified friend, and Chuck Becker on top of the hay wagon. For many years, the big red barn stood in a field on the west side of Sandstone Creek. (Courtesy of Eagle County Historical Society.)

Two

Camp Hale

Although not a contiguous part of Vail Mountain, the large valley due south of Vail was once called Eagle Park. It was also home to a railroad station called Pando. The War Department decided in 1942 that the valley, at an elevation of 9,250 feet with surrounding ridges reaching as high as 13,000 feet, was a perfect place to build a military camp to train recruits for winter warfare.

Construction began in the spring of 1942 and was completed in seven months. Earl Eaton helped build Camp Hale. After the War Department began training skiers in the elite fighting ski corps, it asked the American Ski Patrol Association to contact nationwide ski racing clubs, ski schools, and ski patrol units for possible applicants. Pete Siebert applied and provided the necessary three letters of recommendation.

Camp Hale was active for three years. At its peak, 16,000 soldiers trained at the camp. Winter survival skills were taught alongside experiments in winter survival equipment and clothing. The 10th Mountain Division entered World War II in January 1945 in Italy's northern Apennine Mountains. After a nighttime assault on Riva Ridge, the 10th completely destroyed five elite German divisions. During 114 days of combat, the 10th suffered enormous casualties: 992 killed in action and 4,154 wounded.

After World War II, veterans of the 10th Mountain Division were largely responsible for developing skiing into a popular vacation industry in Colorado. Ex-soldiers from the 10th laid out ski hills, built ski lodges, designed ski lifts, and improved ski equipment. They started ski magazines and opened ski schools. Vail, Aspen, Sugarbush, Crystal Mountain, and Whiteface Mountain are but a few of the ski resorts built by 10th Mountain veterans. Pete Seibert returned to Colorado after the war and met Earl Eaton. Their meeting initiated the vision of building a great ski area, and the mountain lay waiting to be discovered.

As World War II progressed, officials in Washington, DC, and the military debated whether the United States needed an alpine-trained division. Germany had such units, which had established themselves in the Italian Alps. Due to the persistence of Minot Dole, founder of the National Ski Patrol, the decision was made to establish a division of ski troops. The site chosen was the valley at Pando.

At Eagle Park in 1942, construction was underway on the new military camp, which had to be built in seven months. Earl Eaton joined the Civilian Conservation Corps to help build the camp. The plan called for mess halls, barracks, a hospital, a chapel, a fire station, a base exchange, administration buildings, a field house, a stockade, and a guardhouse.

The camp was named for Brig. Gen. Irving Hale, a veteran of the Spanish-American War. Within a month of the construction due date, workers finished the project. Approximately 14,000 of the 16,000 military personal stationed there were members of the 10th Mountain Division.

Recruiters from the National Ski Patrol System brought some of the world's most accomplished skiers to the 10th Mountain Division. Some notable names were Torger Tokel, Friedl Pheifer, Rudy Konieczny, Wendy Cramm, Walter Prager, Percy Rideout, Larry Jump, John Litchfield, and Jacob Nunnemacher. Ski instructors from Mount Hood, the Adirondacks, and Sun Valley also enlisted.

To be accepted into the 10th Mountain Division, applicants had to provide three letters of recommendation. Some recruits knew how to ski, but some did not. Here, high above Camp Hale, soldiers of the 10th Mountain Division practice traveling on skis. While part of their training included downhill skiing, distance training was equally important.

A common training maneuver was a multiday, cross-country trip from Camp Hale to Aspen. Subzero temperatures tested the mettle of the 10th Mountain Division. Canvas tents did little to keep soldiers warm in minus-20-degree temperatures. The soldiers, however, were trained to fight and survive under the most brutal mountain conditions.

Gen. George Price Hays, commander of the 10th Mountain Division, decided that an attack on German-held Mount Belvedere in the Italian Alps would only be successful if German positions on Riva Ridge were captured first. He assigned the task to the 86th Mountain Infantry Regiment, seen here in Italy. For three weeks, the companies planned their attack.

Besides skiing, members of the 10th Mountain Division were trained in rock climbing. On the night of February 18, 1945, companies of the 86th Regiment scaled Riva Ridge on five different locations of the rock wall. Completely taking the Germans by surprise, the 86th Regiment captured Riva Ridge. This image was taken in the Camp Hale area.

The night of February 18, 1945, was moonless. Carrying full equipment (as seen in this photograph taken in Italy), the men silently began their climb up Riva Ridge, which rose 1,700–2,000 feet above the Dardaga River. Two of the five routes up the wall required the use of fixed ropes. Caught unaware, the Germans began ferocious counterattacks, putting the mission in jeopardy. The 10th suffered casualties.

The full white uniform used by 10th Mountain Division soldiers is pictured here. Clarence "Sonny" Hank poses in the Camp Hale area with his seven-foot, three-inch skis. He was in the 126th Engineers as a medical aidman. Clothing for soldiers included wool pants, a jacket, and socks. Tents were made of canvas and were not insulated, but innovative outdoor clothing kept the soldiers warm.

One component of the 10th Mountain Division was the mule train. These animals proved more utilitarian than other types of transport in the mountains. Each mule carried 200 pounds of equipment, supplies, and artillery. Used in Italy, the mules could also easily carry casualties down the mountain. This mule train is in the area of Camp Hale.

While stationed in Camp Hale, members of the 10th Mountain Division were impressed with the terrain and quality of Colorado snow and saw a potential for postwar development. Ski troopers who returned to civilian life, such as Pete Seibert, Bob Parker, "Sarge" Brown, and others, gave birth to Colorado's ski industry.

On the south flank of Mount Terminale, Italy, on March 3, 1945, Pete Seibert had just spoken to Steve Knowlton when Pete heard a deafening blast and saw stars. A mortar shell had exploded in a tree above Pete, and fragments shattered his left forearm and destroyed his kneecap and the top of his femur. A second shell hit him in the chest and the calf of his right leg. Loaded with morphine, Pete made it off the mountain and to the army hospital in Livorno. Two months later, he was in a wheelchair, barely able to feed himself. In October 1945, Pete was well enough to be permitted a weeklong visit home. After another hospital transfer and 10 months of plastic surgeries, Pete was released from the Army in August 1946. He was advised that he might not walk again and certainly would never ski. At that point, all he could do was dream about skiing a powder run, like this unidentified skier in the back bowls at Vail.

Three

THE DISCOVERY ON
NO-NAME MOUNTAIN

As World War II came to a close and Pete Seibert recovered from his war wounds, he worked as a ski patroller and attended a hotel school in Switzerland, eventually returning to Colorado to manage the Loveland Ski Area. Earl Eaton told Pete about a mountain over Vail Pass with treeless back bowls. Interested, Pete agreed to take a look. Before daybreak on March 19, 1957, Pete and Earl snapped into bear-trap bindings, adjusted heavy backpacks, and began to climb what Earl called No-Name Mountain. Using skins on their skis, Pete and Earl embarked on a 3,000-foot vertical ascent in hip-deep snow. The first two miles followed a logging road, and then they entered a dense forest of pine and spruce trees. Two hours later, they emerged on a ridge surrounded by a bowl of trees. Impressed, Pete stopped to catch his breath. Though he did not know it then, he was standing where Mid-Vail would be built.

After a pause for lunch, the men continued their hike to the summit. Traversing a north-south ridge, Pete realized the contours of this mountain matched those of famous European ski resorts. After seven exhausting hours, Pete and Earl reached the summit—11,250 feet above sea level. Pete gulped for air and stopped. Turning in a circle, he saw perfect ski terrain in every direction, the snow sparkling as if littered with diamonds, the sky so blue it seemed fake. Pete glanced at treeless bowls that went on forever. He looked south to the majestic Sawatch Range with the inspirational Mount of the Holy Cross and then north to the jagged skyline of the Gore Range, seemingly glazed with snow. Below him, the pitch of the slope was perfect for skiing. He was speechless. Beside him, Earl leaned on his poles and smiled. Later, when they removed their ski skins and began the descent through champagne powder, there was no doubt that No-Name Mountain was special. Exhausted upon reaching the bottom, Pete and Earl looked over their shoulder.

Both men knew they had found their ski area.

By the late 1950s, some of the early settlers remained along Gore Creek. Although the Greek sheepherders grazed their sheep on the mountain in the summer, it remained largely inaccessible. Large stands of pine mixed with groves of aspen trees covered the front of the mountain, leaving the impression that skiing could only be done after extensive tree cutting.

Raised on a homestead along Squaw Creek, Earl Eaton grew up a dreamer, hunter, hiker, skier, and a man who understood mountains. After high school, Earl joined the Civilian Conservation Crops and then worked on Camp Hale in the 1940s before serving in World War II. After the war, he landed in Aspen and served on the packing crew and ski patrol. He then met Pete Seibert, with whom he shared his dream of finding a ski area.

On March 3, 1945, on Mount Terminale in the Italian Alps, a mortar exploded in the tree next to Pete Seibert. Evacuated from the mountain, Pete spent 17 months in various hospitals while recovering from his wounds. With half a leg blown away, the doctors said he might not walk again and would certainly never ski. Just to prove that no injury would take away his love of skiing, Pete worked hard towards rehabilitation, learned to walk, and eventually learned how to ski again. Because he loved Colorado, he returned, qualified for the 1950 US Ski Team, and joined Aspen's ski patrol. To overcome his damaged leg, Pete would hook his bad leg behind the knee of his good leg and take off down the mountain. (Courtesy of Vail Resorts.)

Different men saw different possibilities when viewing the back bowls of No-Name Mountain. Some saw south-facing slopes, which would mean difficult snow conditions, and wide-open bowls would be a negative factor in Vail's popularity. Seibert and Eaton, however, visualized a winter storm dropping 15 inches of new snow and skiers carving perfect turns without the worry of colliding with a tree. Earl also knew about the snow depths on the mountain because he had placed snow-depth stakes during the summer. Those stakes told him that the mountain averaged over 300 inches of snow per year, and the stakes would end up being useful to the forest service while planning Vail. Those first men who thought the bowls of no consequence were ultimately mistaken.

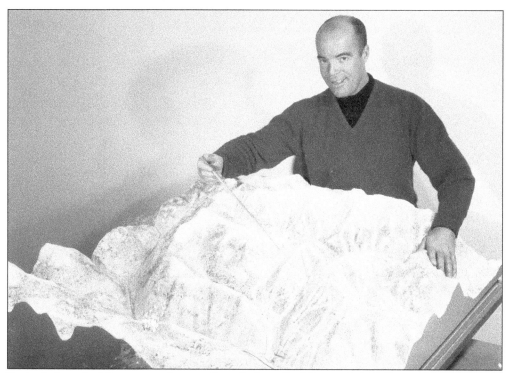

Excited about building a new ski area, Pete Seibert, Earl Eaton, Bob Fuller, and John Conway formed the Transmontane Rod and Gun Club. Each man put up funds to purchase the ranch, with Pete and his wife, Betty, adding the most. Earl Eaton assumed the remaining loan on the property, and John and Bob each put up $7,500. In this photograph, Pete displays a model of No-Name Mountain shown to potential investors.

When the winters became too harsh for the Haas family, they sold their ranch to the Hanson family. John Conway made a point of being friends with John Hanson. Eventually, when cattle prices turned south, Hanson agreed to sell to the Transmontane Rod and Gun Club. This photograph shows Margie Haas with John Berry, who was a barber in Minturn. (Courtesy of the Eagle County Historical Society.)

A portable model of the proposed ski area needed to be constructed to demonstrate the mountain's potential to many prospective investors. George Caulkins and Pete Seibert hit the road with their model to sell limited partnership units to investors. They met with ski clubs, relatives, old school chums, county club friends, and old war buddies—anyone who would listen to Pete's dream of making a ski area out of a sheep pasture. Pete created the original vision and was determined to sell it to enough prospective investors in order to make his dream happen. This photograph shows curator Pam Horan-Kates and former director Don Siminton of the Colorado Ski & Snowboard Museum displaying the model-in-a-box that was built to show early investors. Note there is no Gold Peak or Lionshead area, but Blue Sky Basin is evident.

Four

BUILDING VAIL

Pete Seibert and Earl Eaton had found their mountain. Ten years after the end of World War II, the nation relaxed in times of prosperity and calm. With increased opportunity for recreation, skiing gained popularity as a sport. To build a new ski area, Pete and Earl needed men who could move mountains, but they wanted to do it quietly, because they did not want to escalate real estate prices. The men knew that they needed to acquire the land at the base of No-Name Mountain.

The 520-acre Hanson Ranch encompassed both sides of Highway 6 from the Katsos Ranch in East Vail to what would become West Vail. Teaming with real estate appraiser John Conway and lawyer John Fowler, Pete assigned the job of acquiring the Hanson Ranch to John Conway. Conway introduced himself to John Hanson, explaining how his friends wanted to buy the ranch for hunting and fishing purposes. Hanson was in no mood to sell. From September 1957 to October 1958, Conway became a friendly pest at the Hanson Ranch, stopping by to chat with Hanson, chewing hay, kicking old tires in the yard, and watching the dog chase a squirrel. In the fall of 1958, the price of cattle fell and Hanson was in the mood to sell.

In May 1959, Pete and Earl applied to the US Forest Service for recreational development on Vail Mountain. Due to obligations to Aspen's development, the request was denied. Furious, Pete turned to friendly Colorado congressional representatives. The Forest Service then changed its mind, granting the permit. With the property acquired and permits in place, all the men needed was money to build their resort. Two men, Jack Tweedy and George Caulkins, joined the club. The next step was to find 20 investors, each with $5,000. Investors from eight different states were found. Without having hunted anything or caught anything with fins, the Transmontane Rod and Gun Club was disbanded, and in 1959, the Vail Corporation was formed.

One of the first things the corporation did was choose a name. Once called Pottery Pass from Indian remnants found in the area by English naturalist Dru Lison Cockerell in 1888, and then called Mill Creek-Two Elk Creek area by a forester, the region was referred to by others as the Vail Pass Area after Charlie Vail. One man suggested that the mountain be named Shining Mountain, the name the Ute Indians had for the area, but Pete thought that when mountains shone, it meant they were icy, and he nixed the idea. Finally, the name *Vail* was chosen since it was short and conveyed a valley. This photograph shows the original aerial view of the first proposed lifts. Visible are the proposed gondola, chairlift number two to the top of the mountain, the back-bowls chairlift, and a proposed T-bar.

Earl Eaton had been up and down Vail Mountain on foot, skis, and in his Kristi Kat. It became the vehicle that transported prospective investors to the top of Vail Mountain for a look at the bowls and usually a picnic during nice weather. In this photograph, Earl (left), Pete Seibert (right), and an unidentified visitor cruise the ridge above the back bowls.

An early conceptual design for Vail Village shows the covered bridge and a curved Bridge Street. The original concept was for a European, alpine-feeling village. In 1960 and 1961, Fitzhugh Scott was instrumental in providing ideas, designs, and enthusiasm for the village. Without a deed, Fitzhugh built the first chalet in the village.

In the spring of 1962, construction began on the village and lifts. Due to a wet spring, every depression turned into a mud hole. Leonard Ruder somehow graded a road to Mid-Vail. Earl Eaton and his team cleared trails and built lifts. A jungle of trailers provided housing for workers. In the photograph, a lone sign announces Vail.

When construction began at Vail, conditions were primitive. There was no grocery store, Laundromat, fire department, doctor, veterinarian, pharmacy, television, radio, or gas station. Telephone service was an eight-party line that worked best after 10 o'clock at night. Because of these conditions, everyone had natural concern for others. (Courtesy of Barry Stott/Stott Shot.)

In the early years, newcomers arrived in town for a few ski days and stayed for a lifetime. Everyone had one thing in common—he or she hailed from some other place. Confirmed ski bums mixed with Boston blue bloods, cowboys, bankers, lawyers, and CFOs of huge companies. With no social classes to divide the newcomers, they easily formed bonds. Streets were still dirt. (Courtesy of Sandy Hinmon.)

This photograph from the fall of 1962 shows Vail Mountain. Two hundred plumbers, electricians, and carpenters worked on the mountain and lived in trailers. The gondola towers were shipped to Vail from a Houston dock and installed at tilted, perpendicular angles. Huge spools of high-tension wire were strung between the towers.

One day in October, Earl Eaton and his crew had finished stringing cable for the back-bowls lift. At lunch, they moved to a grassy spot. Suddenly, the clamps on the cable broke. One mile of cable whipped down the slope, wrapping around a lift tower. The tower ripped from its foundation and sailed 200 yards down the hill. Fortunately, no one was hurt.

Despite the use of modern machinery, the builders of Vail's lifts still often relied on men and muscle power to erect and test them. Because weight limit was not an exact science, this photograph shows the lift crew loading bags of sand to test the weight limits of the newly installed chairlift.

Trail cutting was not an exact science, either. However, Pete had a wonderful logic of a mountain slope and how the run should be cleared, as evidenced by Riva Ridge and how it is now. Because of Pete's incredible skiing sense, he could stand in the middle of an uncut trail and knew how it should be cut without modern GPS technology. (Courtesy of Vail Resorts.)

Originally built in the summer of 1962, Mid-Vail was a modest flat-roofed building with a sprawling sundeck and stunning views of the Gore Range. The more recognizable second story with expansive windows was added later. As late as December 15 of the opening season, cars were able to drive to Mid-Vail due to its lack of snow. (Courtesy of Barry Stott/Stott Shot.)

First to see the mountain with Pete Seibert in Earl Eaton's Kristi Kat in 1957, Bob Parker was awed by what he saw. A 10th Mountain Division recruit, Parker served as an intelligence scout for the 87th Mountain Regiment. After more schooling, another three-year stint in the US Army, ski racing, ski patrolling, and more years in the military, he became editor of *Skiing* magazine from 1956–1962. When that job ended, Bob joined Pete in Vail. His first job was to restructure components of the Bell gondola due to be delivered in February. Since Vail would open in December, Parker had to scramble to reorganize delivery in time for opening day. Bob was the principal founder of the Vail Ski Museum, later named the Colorado Ski & Snowboard Museum. (Courtesy of Vail Resorts.)

Mid-Vail became the place to start the day, the place to stop for lunch, the place to people watch, and the place to be seen. With an awesome view of the infamous Look Ma Run, which held ski competitions, and with its generous decks for sun worshippers, Mid-Vail instantly became popular. It started as one cafeteria-style restaurant. After various remodels and additions, it now contains four different restaurants. (Courtesy of Betty Josey.)

Although Pete Seibert had connections in the ski business world, Earl Eaton did not. On the other hand, Earl could build things, fix things, and made sure that Vail's lifts were installed properly. Here, Earl (left) takes a break inside the main Vail gondola terminal with an unidentified coworker. He had a job with a superb view. (Courtesy of Vail Resorts.)

The Rocky Mountains are still relatively young. Millions of years of ocean flooding, glacial valleys, fractures, and upheavals formed the mountains. Both the Gore and Sawatch Ranges are faulted anticlines, and Vail Mountain was formed from deposits. For the mountain, weather comes A blizzards, gentle snowfalls, rain, hail, mist, fog, and sunshine. Here, a cloud leaves a Vail street in haze the late 1960s.

By 1879, white men had driven the Ute Indians out of Colorado. In 1962, Bob Parker invited the Utes back to the Gore Valley. With Vail due to open in six days and with scant snow, Parker called Eddie Box (left) from the Bear Clan of the Southern Ute Tribe. Eddie then sought council with Minnie Cloud of the Cloud Clan, because Minnie's specialty was bringing rain. An unidentified dancer is at right.

Minnie Cloud of the Ute Cloud Clan agreed to perform a rain dance with some modification to make it a snow dance. On December 9, 1962, a dozen Ute dancers arrived, guided by Eddie and Minnie. They danced at the Lodge and Mid-Vail. Under clear skies, the Ute dancers departed on December 11, 1962. Vail opened on December 15, and a blizzard hit on December 17. The Ute have not had to perform another snow dance for Vail. As the years passed, Vail seeded the clouds to ensure snowfall. At one point, Allen Nottingham flew his plane over Vail and poured table salt out the plane window to seed the clouds. He only did this once.

After a few years, Vail continued to grow. In this photograph, Wall Street is being graded for construction. Vail's success in its early years was due to the condominium concept, popularity of air travel, revolutions in ski equipment, comfortable and warm ski clothing, and the Bogner look, which brought fashion to the slopes. (Courtesty of Sandy Himon.)

The first lift ticket office in Vail was a six-sided building between the gondola and Dick Hauserman's Gondola Ski Shop. Ticket sellers carried the day's receipts to the Vail Associates office in a brown paper shopping bag. In the foreground of this photograph is the Mill Creek Court building. Earl Eaton's son Carl was the first baby born in Vail, in the clinic in that building.

For the first 10 years or so, people called the spring months "Mud Season"—and for good reason. When Vail was incorporated, it had minimal funds for improvements, and several bond issues were passed by the five or six permanent residents of Vail to provide a water and sanitation district. Still, the roads were not paved. During the midwinter months, the ground froze and mud was not a problem, but come spring, the snow melted and turned the rich topsoil into a thick brown ooze of mud. In ski boots, people trudged through the mud to the lifts and back to the parking lots. Day skiers left the muck behind, but locals lived with it in the spring. In this photograph of Gore Creek Drive in the late 1960s, the roads are being graded for paving. (Courtesy of Sandy Hinmon.)

GORSUCH LTD.

Two members of the US Ski Team, Dave and Renie Gorsuch, drove from their ski shop in Gunnison to take a look at Vail. Upon retiring from ski racing and ready for a change, Dave and Renie decided to put down roots in Vail. They opened Gorsuch Limited in the new Clock Tower building, which was built by John and Lorrie McBride.

With six locations throughout Colorado, Gorsuch stores continue to delight customers. The company's catalog division is now in its 36th year and sends out millions of copies spotlighting mountain living in Vail. Here is a photograph of one page of the first Gorsuch catalog, which was produced in 1967. Bogner ski apparel is just as timely today as it was then. (Courtesy of Renie Gorsuch.)

Pepi Gramshammer, a professional ski racer and former cheesemaker from Austria, came to America in 1960. After visiting Vail, he decided to stay. He met Sheika Moser in Aspen in 1962. Dashing and personable, Pepi wooed Sheika, a gorgeous Las Vegas dancer who had never been on a pair of skis. They became engaged in December 1963. (Courtesy of Vail Resorts.)

Everyone in Vail opened his or her arms to Sheika Moser. Pepi Gramshammer, however, had not confirmed a wedding date. Sheika decided on February 3, 1964—right after a race in Aspen. When she informed him, he demurred, and she was ready to end the relationship. Despite this, they got married in Aspen with a reception at Guido's and another party that night in Vail. (Courtesy of Barry Stott/Stott Shot.)

While Sheika trained in the hotel business, Gastoff Gramshammer was built in the summer of 1964. The building included a hotel, sports shop, nightclub, and restaurant. Pepi and Sheika continue to greet visitors and call people from all over the world their friends. Both have been ambassadors for Vail and helped bring the FIS (Fédération Internationale de Ski) Alpine World Ski Championships to Vail's door. (Courtesy of Barry Stott/Stott Shot.)

In the early days of Vail, John Donovan (right) lived with Paul Testwuide (left) in a condominium over the liquor store. Back in those days, it was a wild group, but times changed. John taught skiing and then became a ski school supervisor and a member of the town council. Paul worked for the ski patrol and became ski patrol director in 1974, later working for Vail Associates as chief executive. (Courtesy of Diana Donovan.)

Five

THE EARLY YEARS

During Vail's opening year, 1962, a lift ticket cost $5. The ski school's first director was Morrie Sheppard, and he had eight contract instructors and three supervisors. Pepi Gramshammer was hired as ski school ambassador, and to this day remains an ambassador for Vail. In 1965, Roger Staub from Arosa, Switzerland, was appointed the new ski school director. Staub has appeared in many promotional films, always wearing his white wool cap with a visor. From a simple beginning of contract instructors, the ski school has grown to be a major part of resort operation, with over 1,500 instructors who are fluent in numerous languages.

Vail Mountain needed a ski patrol, so Morrie recruited Don Almond, a detail-orientated man from Aspen. Under his leadership, Vail's became a model for other ski patrols to follow. Six patrolmen started in 1962, and others joined the following year, including Paul Testwuide, Dickie Peterson, Dick Dennison, and Sandy Hinmon, just to name a few who left lasting impressions. Others arrived who created a lasting mark on Vail, such as the Staufers, Hausermans, Dobsons, Burdicks, Gramshammers, Gorsuches, Laziers, Langmaids, McBrides, Schobers, and Bill Whiteford, among many others.

Conditions at the time were still primitive. The streets were dirt, and there was no grocery store, no pharmacy, no animal control, and no radio or television. Telephone service was sketchy at best. Any serious medical problem had to be transported to Glenwood Springs or Denver. Housing for workers remained a problem. Vail had one gas station. By 1966, Vail Associates was unable to continue managing both the town and the mountain, so the town incorporated. The first mayor was Ted Kindal, and the first town manager was Blake Lynch. At the time, Vail did not have much, but it did have the most important aspects of a mountain town: snow and skiers.

Joe Fear, a resident of Red Cliff since 1929, operated the only gas station in town, the Conoco station next to the Vail Village Inn. This 1962 photograph shows Joe as he helps a customer fill her car after a day of skiing. Note the size of her skis. (Courtesy of the Eagle County Historical Society.)

When the US Forest Service issued a recreational permit for Vail, the area was required to have at least 30 sleeping rooms in place. Thus, the Lodge at Vail (seen here shortly after completion) was built. The night it opened its doors for business in 1962, the paint was still wet on the walls. The opening night party required coat-and-tie dress attire. (Courtesy of Barry Stott/Stott Shot.)

With no experience, Charlie Gersbach was named the first manager of the Vail Village Inn, seen in the lower right-hand corner. The inn also acted as the bus stop and had the town's only gas station. At the opening day event, Charlie had to contend with a broken water pipe that poured water over the banquet table. Charlie lasted one year at the inn—but decades more in Vail.

When Mid-Vail first opened, it was the center of all activity on Vail Mountain. Lift-line mazes were constructed from tall poles and ropes. With two-person chairlifts that were not high-speed, waiting in lift lines—especially during holiday season—could be a lengthy process. This 1960s-era photograph shows Chair 4. (Courtesy of Diana Donovan.)

Pictured behind the bar is Bill Whiteford, known as a loveable scoundrel. Without permit or license, Bill built his Ice Bar outside of Mid-Vail in 1964. It was a full-service bar that served sandwiches and soup. Vail Associates would shut him down, and he would reopen. Finally, the US Forest Service closed the bar down permanently due to Bill's advertising Carpano on the outdoor umbrella. (Courtesy of Betty Josey.)

In the 1960s, Bill Whiteford built the Casino, which he claimed was the largest discotheque in the country at one time. He had all kinds of entertainment—Dizzy Gillespie, folksingers, jazz bands, and others. Saturday nights were the wildest. Then, on Sunday mornings, amidst cigarette fumes and empty beer glasses, Fr. Tom Stone held mass at 8:00 a.m.

Now that Vail was actually a town, mail needed to be delivered. The first post office started in the deli, moved below the Gorsuch building, and then relocated to Crossroads. After operating where the town offices are today, it finally moved to its current location on Frontage Road. Diana Donovan is shown here in the mid-1960s after picking up her mail from the deli. (Courtesy of Diana Donovan.)

Morrie Shepard, Vail's first ski school director, grew up with Pete Seibert in Sharon, Massachusetts. Both worked together at the Aspen Ski School. Besides being the ski school director, Morrie worked on trails in the summer. He was also fire chief and building inspector. Morrie left as director in 1965. (Courtesy of Vail Resorts.)

After Morrie Shepard left in 1965, Roger Staub (pictured) took over the ski school. Roger, a native of Switzerland, won a gold medal in the Squaw Valley Winter Olympics in 1960. Always dressed in a white wool cap, he was filmed extensively for Vail's promotional material. Roger was instrumental in recruiting top-notch instructors, who developed the ski school into one of the foremost in the world. After becoming director of skiing, Roger lived in the Clock Tower building next door to John Donovan and roommate Paul Testwuide. The three eligible and charismatic men kept the Clock Tower building a lively place. Sadly, Roger died in a hang gliding accident a few years later in Switzerland. (Courtesy of Barry Stott/Stott shot.)

Skiers had to know which runs were open and which were closed. No lighted boards or grooming reports were used in the early years. Instead, this information board was displayed at the bottom of Pepi's Face. The Open and Closed signs had to be changed manually.

Although most attention was given to downhill skiing when Vail first opened, Steve Rieschl convinced those running the ski school to add a ski-touring division. Steve ran that branch of the ski school and should be remembered as the man responsible for increasing the popularity of the sport in Vail and elsewhere.

Pictured is the Rucksack, the "have everything" store at the time it opened in the mid-1960s. Although cars could park on the dirt streets in the early days, people also rode into town on their horses to get the mail, buy a cold drink, or see Ted Poliak, the pharmacist. (Courtesy of Barry Stott/Stott Shot.)

Antsy for change, Larry Burdick came to Vail and opened the Red Lion in February 1963. Larry intended to open a small photo shop in the building, but he instead leased the space to the Vail Clinic. The Red Lion became a trademark in Vail and still is. Larry married Marge Walsh, and another Vail love story began. They were active in many causes that made Vail successful. (Courtesy of Barry Stott/Stott Shot.)

In the 1960s, the ski school continued to grow. By the winter of 1967–1968, it expanded from the original eight instructors to 40, as shown in this photograph. In 1983, the *Vail Trail* newspaper ran a contest to see who could name all the instructors in the photograph. The winner was awarded a ski lesson. (Courtesy of Diana Donovan.)

During Vail's first season, the mountain hosted the US Olympic Training Camp. Skiing stars such as Billy Kidd, Jimmy Huega, Suzie Chaffee, Spider Sabich, Buddy Werner, and the Ferries trained at the camp. Correspondents began to send nationwide news flashes about Vail and how the racers endured subzero temperatures during camp. (Courtesy of Barry Stott/ Stott Shot.)

Pete Seibert and Bob Parker knew from the start that big-time ski racing would be an integral part of Vail's image. Beginning in 1964, Vail was one of the few American ski resorts to host international ski races. Those spectators at the finish line were thrilled to see the likes of Billy Kidd, Karl Schranz, and Jean-Claude Killy fly over Pepi's Face on International. (Courtesy of Barry Stott/Stott Shot.)

In January 1963, Pete Seibert initiated the first Vail Cup, a training exercise for the major races of the future and proof that Vail could anchor a major event. In 1965, Vail held its first international race, matching the great alpine ski teams of Europe against those of Canada and the United States. The races were held in 1965, 1967, and 1969.

In the early 1960s, Vail was a regular stop on the hotdog skiing circuit. Bump contests and aerial competitions took place on Look Ma, which wowed the crowds watching from Mid-Vail and the lift lines. The events set the stage for modern freestyle skiing. The jumper shown here is getting big air and looks as though he could fly.

People began to hear about Vail, although some had difficulty with directions because many rental car agencies had never heard of it. However, by Vail's third ski season, the area claimed more skier days than any other Colorado ski area. By its fifth ski season, it managed 250 percent of its initial projections. A lift ticket in 1964 cost $6.50 on the weekends.

Vail Village continued to prosper along with the mountain. More buildings were constructed, including the Plaza and the Red Lion. The intersection of Meadow Drive and Bridge Street became a hub of activity. By 1966, Vail Associates decided it could no longer run both the mountain and the town, so the Town of Vail incorporated that same year. (Courtesy of Sandy Hinmon.)

In the late 1960s, people had to entertain themselves since television service was limited. In the summertime, Vail held Wild West Days. Guys and girls could dress like mountain men and women and display their skills with black powder rifles, ax throwing, or whatever else they could dream up. Chuck Malloy, Dickie Pete, Phil Kirchbaum, and Mike Tennett are among the mountain men seen here. (Courtesy of Sandy Hinmon.)

After Vail incorporated, Ted Kindal, who built the Christiana Lodge, became the first mayor. In 1967, John Dobson took over as mayor for eight years. John and Cissy Dobson moved to Vail from Vermont and built the Covered Bridge Store on Bridge Street in 1965. To validate the store name, they paid half of the cost of construction for the covered bridge.

It quickly became evident that Vail needed its own doctor. Those first years, injured patients were taken to Aspen, Glenwood, or Denver. In 1965, Dr. Tom Steinberg and his wife, Flo, arrived in Vail. His first office was in the kitchen of the Red Lion; next, he had offices in the Mill Creek Court building where the X-ray room was built too small to move a gurney. Doctor Steinberg therefore had to carry his patients to the X-ray room. (Courtesy of Tom Steinberg.)

By 1965, new trails and lifts had been built. Don Almond was the mountain manager, but he needed help. With an invitation by Pete Seibert (left) and Bob Parker (center) to come to Vail, Bill Brown (right) arrived to town. At the time, he was a sergeant training ROTC recruits at Dartmouth. Bill worked with the trail crew and said half of the time he could not find them. He ended up firing most of the crew and starting over. From then on, he was called "Sarge." Throughout the next few seasons, Sarge cleaned up the ski patrol. The group was a hard-drinking bunch used to high jinks on the mountain, but Sarge got that under control. Eventually, he became the mountain manager after Don Almond left in 1970. Sarge left his imprint with Pete Seibert and Bob Parker by running many championship races on Vail Mountain, the pinnacle being the FSI World Alpine Ski Championships in 1989. Here, the three men stand behind the sign for Minnie's Mile, a run named for Minot Dole, who founded the National Ski Patrol.

Mountains make men, and men make legends. Paul Testwuide is a legend in Vail. Paul and John Donovan were roommates and knew how to make their own fun. The town was raw and wooly, and Paul said that every night was Saturday night in Vail—and Saturday night in Vail was like New Year's Eve. Paul is on the right in this photograph, and Sarge Brown is on the left. (Courtesy of Vail Resorts.)

John Donovan bought La Cave's Copper Bar and turned it into Donovan's Copper Bar. For many years, it was the après-ski hangout for ski patrol, ski school, and workers. Many wives called John at the bar and asked him to relay messages to their spouses. If it got really busy, John pulled someone behind the bar and put them to work. No one minded; it was Donovan's. (Courtesy of Diana Donovan.)

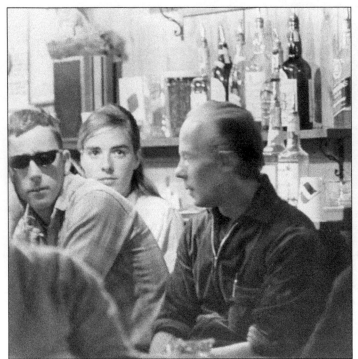

Donovan's was one place that had a television. For any important news or sports event, most locals gathered there. However, no one dared to tell John to turn off a Notre Dame football game. Here, John, Diana Donovan, and Bob Porter sit quietly during the historic moon landing of Apollo 11. The bar was packed, and hardly anyone spoke. (Courtesy of Diana Donovan.)

Donovan's was the place to be on St. Patrick's Day. Green beer, Dynamite Dogs, and pretzels were served. John planned accordingly with ample kegs of beer. In 1982, John lost his lease on the bar and the last drop of beer was poured at Donovan's. John continued to work with the ski school and was a town council member for 16 years. (Courtesy of Diana Donovan.)

After a sun-kissed day on the slopes, skiers moseyed to the back deck at Donovan's. Beer cost 35¢ a glass. If someone only had a quarter, John would drink 10¢ worth and then hand over the glass. When Vail Associates did not give the ski patrollers a raise, John did so in the form of a free beer. To this day, John remains the longest-serving employee of Vail Resorts. (Courtesy of Diana Donovan.)

Vail welcomes its one-millionth skier. In 1968, Sally Warren and her husband began a midday of skiing. When Sally bought her ski ticket, she was stopped and told that she was the one-millionth skier. In addition to a key to the town, she got a pair of Head 360 model, 195-centimeter skis.

As Vail prospered, the mountain continued to grow. First came the addition of Golden Peak, which included Chair 12 and Chair 6. To the right of Chair 6 is the infamous run BooBoo, gleaning its name from the 30-foot-wide trail cut to the top of Golden Peak that was never used. The base area provided a wonderful spot to rest and watch skiers. (Courtesy of Sandy Hinmon.)

High jinks, moonlight skiing in the back bowls, the Tuck-Em-Inn, and closing the Casino in the wee hours of the morning were not the only things the ski patrol members were known to do. Ski patrolman Dozer Johnson decided to prove it possible to drive his Jeep off the China Bowl wall one summer day in the late 1960s and lived to tell about it. (Courtesy of Don Johnson.)

In the 1960s, the term "ski-in, ski-out" applied to most everyone who lived on Forest and Rockledge Roads. Pictured are Betty Josey and Elaine Kelton (riding sidekick) as they head down the road to begin an après-ski party. Betty has Head metal skis, Bogner stretch pants, leather buckle boots, and a white wool Sherpa hat. (Courtesy of Betty Josey.)

With more terrain to cover, Vail introduced snowmobiles to Vail Mountain. In this photograph, ski patrolman Dickie Pete shows off the first snowmobile to be used on the slopes; he is pulling a couple of fellow patrolman who are not visible. The snowmobile made transportation easier for ski patrol, race crews, lift operators, and maintenance men. (Courtesy of Sandy Hinmon.)

The Lodge at Vail was the place to be in the early days, whether it was for a ski vacation or summer fun. Trained in hotel and restaurant service in Switzerland and Germany, Joe Stauffer arrived in Vail after having difficulty finding it. His first night in town was spent at the Avon Country Store in a room with a light bulb on a string. In 1963, Joe Stauffer was the Lodge's second manager, and in 1964, he managed Mid-Vail. In a few short years, Joe went from Lodge manager to becoming a major partner in real estate and restaurant management. Although Joe became involved with hotels and restaurants, he got his start in America at the Lodge and made it profitable. The Lodge remains a favorite hotel in both the winter and summer. (Courtesy of Barry Stott/Stott Shot.)

Six

NOW A SKI TOWN

In the beginning, when Vail Mountain needed a ski patrol, Morrie Shepard recruited Don Almond, a detail-orientated man from Aspen. Under his leadership, Vail's became a model for other ski patrols to follow. Six patrolmen started in 1962, with others following the next year. Steve Reichl, a ski instructor, was also an expert in cross-county and telemark skiing, eventually running that division of the ski school. Don Almond managed lift operators and groomers.

An injured skier was taken to Aspen to see Dr. Bob Oden, the only orthopedist on the Western Slope. A medical office of sorts was located in the Red Lion, and then office space was built in the Plaza Building. For non-mountain injuries, people could go to Gilman and see Doctor Stanley, whose patients were mainly from the Gilman Mine. More serious medical needs were transported to Glenwood Springs or Denver. By 1965, Dr. Thomas Steinberg was treating his first patients in town.

Vail Country Day School opened in 1963, with four students and Allen Brown as headmaster. In 1965, George Knox produced Vail's first newspaper, the *Vail Trail*. There were restaurants and, of course, Donovan's Copper Bar, the most famous watering hole in town. At the bar the Slope, a person could relax on the thickly carpeted floor, watch ski movies, and have a beer. Yes, Vail had become a town.

Pres. Gerald Ford was the first skiing president, and some believe he was the most rugged man to occupy the White House. Since 1966, the Ford family has vacationed in Vail. Once Ford was president, the family resided in the Richard Bass residence on Mill Creek Circle. Richard Bass had built the biggest house—with 35-foot ceilings—on Mill Creek Circle. The Secret Service and White House staff members used four neighboring homes. Manor Vail accommodated the press staff and supplied a briefing room. The above 1974 photograph shows President Ford (left) greeting Don Welch, a ski school supervisor. When the president had skied as vice president, he did not cut lift lines. As president, he did. In the left photograph, President Ford (center), Bob Parker (right), and Richard Bass examine vintage hickory skis, while Secret Servicemen carefully watch from the background. (Above, courtesy of Don Welch.)

Some of the early residents were middle-aged dropouts from more civilized occupations, such as stockbrokers, bankers, and executives from big corporations and bigger cities. These people needed a change and found it in the fledgling mountain town. They also found that they could be part of something wonderful. This photograph was used for advertising purposes in *Western Skier*. The ad states, "Where else could you hire all these experts for $93 a week? Vail, the complete ski area, offered ski patrolmen, ski instructors, pharmacists, bartenders, maitre d's, lift operators, hair dressers, chefs, policemen, firemen, doctors, dogs, and much more, all waiting to serve. From Ted Kindel, Bill Duddy, Shirley Ward, to Sarge Brown, John Russell and others, they all were happy be part of Vail's Ski Weeks." (Courtesy of Barry Stott/Stott Shot.)

Some of the first residents who came to Vail did so for the adventure of building something from nothing. The next wave of residents arrived in Vail to benefit from the town's booming success. During the 1970s, the noise of bulldozers and hammers was incessant. Condominiums popped up like weeds. Here is Diana Donovan with Bandit in front of Manor Vail. (Courtesy of Diana Donovan.)

In 1974, Vail's police force was eight years old. Pictured are police officers Jack Haynes, Craig Wright, Russ Motta, Dave Bustos, and friends taking a break from keeping law and order. In 1968, police chief Ted Holms and four others were taken hostage by attempted robbers at the Lodge. Left handcuffed to a tree on Vail Pass, Chief Holms uprooted the tree and escaped. (Courtesy of the Vail Police Department.)

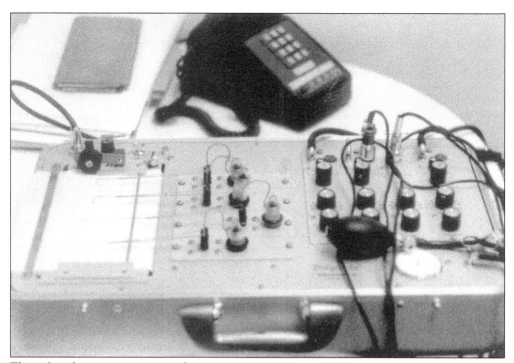

The police department ran on a slim budget in the early years. If a crime had been committed that required the suspect to take a lie-detector test, the police department had to scramble. Finally, the Vail police found an airline pilot who flew in and out of Eagle County and was qualified to administer lie-detector tests. This was the machine he used for those tests. (Courtesy of Vail Police Department.)

Police work meant more than giving tickets for cars parked in no-parking zones. Tenacious bears emerged from hibernation, and some found a way into local homes.Here is policeman Mark Allen removing a pesky cub for relocation to a better bear cub habitat. The bear was successfully relocated. (Courtesy of Vail Police Department.)

The Vail Police Department began a 25-year Saab story when it adopted the Swedish automaker's vehicles as its official patrol cars. Providing speed and maneuverability, Saabs also fitted a fashion trend that patrons demanded. The officers loved to drive them as well. In this photograph, officer Pat McCullough heads for his patrol car in 1980. (Courtesy of the Vail Police Department.)

Although not a contiguous part of Vail, Piney Lake with its majestic beauty has been part of the valley from the early years. Before Vail was settled, Piney was a destination spot for fishermen, honeymoons, and outdoor enthusiasts. At an elevation of 9,400 feet, it still inspires visitors with panoramic views, hiking, fishing, and camping. (Courtesy of Barry Stott/Stott Shot.)

For many years in the spring, the ski patrol played the ski school during a softball game at Golden Peak. Beer drinking was required. The annual event was started by John Donovan and continued for many years. Some years, it was played in a snowstorm, as shown in this photograph from the early 1970s. (Courtesy of Sandy Hinmon.)

While being a ski patrolman seemed glamorous, it actually demanded a lot of long hours and offered low pay. Yes, the patrolmen had to know how to ski, but they were also trained in evacuation, as shown in this photograph from the late 1960s. Here, patrol members practice evacuating a victim out of the back bowls via Chair 5, onto Chair 4, and down to Mid-Vail. (Courtesy of Sandy Hinmon.)

Early morning avalanche patrol meant spending the night at patrol headquarters, building bombs, sipping beer, and starting up the lifts for a powder run in the back bowls. In the morning, the patrollers were out on skis before anyone else, setting off avalanche charges. (Courtesy of Sandy Hinmon.)

As Vail prospered, so did the members of the ski school. In the early days, guys wore blue parkas and the girls wore yellow parkas. Seen here are the members of the Vail Ski School in the early 1970s, posing for a photograph, with some on the roof of the Golden Peak building. The ski school locker room was on the ground floor of the building.

Jebbie Brown (second row, far right) taught every local child in Vail and kept mothers sane. In the early days, children could be dropped off in the morning with Jebbie and picked up at Donovan's Copper Bar at the end of the day. In this 1975 photograph, Jebbie is seen with helper Sandi Brenden (far left). Among the young skiers are Vanessa White, Michael Freeman, John Donovan, and Dana Dawson. (Courtesy of Jebbie Brown.)

In the days of two-person ski lifts, Jebbie and two toddlers fit nicely. Lift attendants helped her organize the children and get them lined up as the chairlift approached, but Jebbie had to keep them on the chair. Note that gloves did not fit properly, and no one cared. In this 1978 photograph, Jebbie is seen with Brian Buckley (left) and Ryan Welch. (Courtesy of Jebbie Brown.)

In the winter season of 1974–1975, Vail recorded an outstanding 456 inches of snow. People call it "champagne powder" for a reason, and Rocky Mountain powder is some of the driest and lightest in the world. In the early years, untracked powder could be found for days. This is Walt Olsen at Chair 5. (Courtesy of Sandy Hinmon.)

In this 1970s-era photograph, ski school instructors ride the bumps on Vail Mountain. Certain slopes were not groomed purposely, so bump enthusiasts would be delighted. As more skiers took up the sport, moguls skiing became a coveted skill and eventually a competitive discipline in the Olympics.

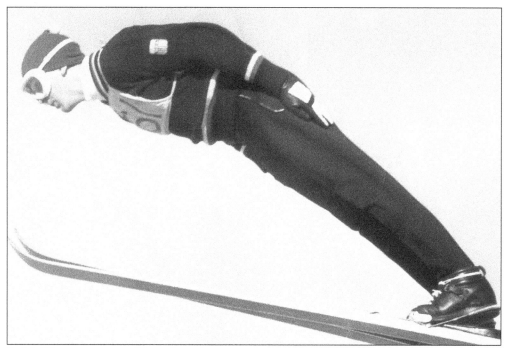

Buddy Werner, a native of Steamboat Springs, was an internationally renowned Nordic and alpine ski racer. He was a member of the 1956, 1960, and 1964 US Olympic Alpine teams. He died in an avalanche in 1964 while filming in Europe, but Buddy left an imprint on many young Vail skiers. Here, Buddy shows perfect form with a long jump.

Founded in 1960, the Buddy Werner League is a recreational ski race club for young skiers with volunteer coaches. There are leagues all over the United States. Many young racers in Vail began their career in the Buddy Werner League. This photograph shows Patrick Welch competing in a Buddy Werner race in 1985.

In the late 1960s and early 1970s, the Front Range Polar Bear Ski Club bused young skiers to Vail on Saturdays. Polar Bear classes were not allowed to cut the lift lines, thus instructors kept their classes on the front side of the mountain, skiing Giant Steps and International. The Polar Bear kids became expert spring-snow skiers.

Vail continued to grow. Skiing was now a glamorous sport. In Vail's third season, it counted more skier days than any other Colorado resort. Pictured here in the 1960s is Bridge Street, before the days of heated streets.

With limited television service in town, telephones still archaic, only a few restaurants, and no churches or recreation centers, the only thing to do on a lazy sunny morning in the 1960s was to sit on the bench outside the Gorsuch building. At that time, the upstairs was living quarters. Pictured are, from left to right, Clay Freeman, unidentified, Chupa Nelson, and two unidentified friends. (Courtesy of Sandy Hinmon.)

John Donovan met Diana Mounsey in Vail, and they announced their engagement in the Copper Bar in 1967. By the time they had children, the town had few preschools. In this photograph, Diana demonstrates a typical day on the slopes with toddlers in tow. Diana Donovan served years on the Vail Town Council. Kerry Donovan, Diana's daughter, serves on the council today. (Courtesy of Diana Donovan.)

Jimmie Heuga became one of the first two members of the men's US Ski Team to win an Olympic medal. In 1958, at age 15, he was the youngest man to make the team. Jimmie won a bronze medal in the slalom in the 1964 Winter Olympics. Retiring to Vail, he was diagnosed with multiple sclerosis in 1970. He founded the Heuga Center for Multiple Sclerosis in Edwards, which has helped thousands of people overcome the symptoms of the disease. Today, the center has been renamed Can Do MS and continues to be an advocate of exercise and activity to combat the disease. Jimmie left a legacy and was an inspiration for all skiers.

Pres. Gerald and Betty Ford were not the only notables who vacationed in Vail. The Edward Kennedy family, shown above in the 1960s, enjoyed skiing trips to Vail as well. In 1973, 12-year-old Teddy Kennedy was looking forward to the Christmas vacation in Vail. Instead, his leg was amputated due to bone cancer. Four months later, he was on Vail's slopes. Vail was chosen because of the moderate slopes and because privacy was not hard to achieve. It did not take long for Teddy to get the hang of skiing again, using outrigger poles and with Blair Ammons as his instructor. In March 1968, Jacqueline Kennedy also visited Vail with Caroline. They are pictured at right in Vail Village just prior to stepping out and shopping before their ski vacation began. Vail was always happy to welcome VIPs, and locals and tourists alike respected their privacy. (Both, courtesy of Barry Stott/Stott Shot.)

The first trail groomers on Vail Mountain were John Carnie's foot groomers. John and his crew of four would head up the mountain on skis with a shovel. They would ski to the worst bumps, shovel off the tops, dump the snow in the valley, then flatten the snow with their skis. Later, grooming progressed to grooming machines, as seen here.

As grooming improved, skiers became accustomed to "corduroy" snow, where the grooming operator has laid down a perfect run of snow. Today, Vail is famous for grooming runs during the day. This grooming operator drives a BP600 Winch with a price tag of about $350,000. On a given day, Vail runs between 18 and 24 machines. (Courtesy of Barry Stott/Stott Shot.)

In the early years, the back bowls (pictured) would keep powder hounds happy for three days before it became packed. The first bowls were Sun Up and Sun Down Bowls, with Game Creek Bowl added later. It was Pepi Gramshammer who named the run Forever after skiing it before any lifts were installed and saying, "It took forever to climb out of there." (Courtesy of Barry Stott/Stott Shot.)

In 1969, Vail Associates took over a plot of ground west of the main village that was used as a rock gravel operation. The company borrowed the name *Lionshead* from the rock outcropping due south of the area, which overlooked the old railroad and mining town of Minturn. A ski lift ticket that year cost $8.

Born Free and Simba were the first two trails cut in Lionshead. The area also opened up Game Creek Bowl on the backside of the mountain. A new gondola was built, which whisked people from the base to Eagle's Nest with its stunning views. The new village at Lionshead was built in a more modern tradition. (Courtesy of Barry Stott/Stott Shot.)

Opened in 1969 with a six-passenger gondola and Chair 7 in Game Creek Bowl, Lionshead added over three square miles of ski terrain to Vail Mountain. Later, Chairs 8 and 9 were added alongside the gondola and a children's Poma Lift was built at the top. Eagle's Nest provided another on-mountain restaurant facility with jaw-dropping views.

In order to build the lifts on the backside of Lionshead area into what was called Game Creek Bowl, a road was cut down the run Showboat. On the right is a run called Lost Boy. On the left is Ouzo, named for the Greek liqueur the sheepherders liked to sip to ward off a chilly night. (Courtesy of Barry Stott/Stott Shot.)

The first crisis to hit Vail Mountain was when Martin Koether, age 14, got lost in unopened Game Creek Bowl before it was developed. Searchers spent the night looking for him. Although tired and hungry, he was found safely, and the run Lost Boy is named after him. In this photograph, his aunt, Mrs. Herbert Koether, greets him. (Courtesy of Barry Stott/Stott Shot; photograph by Dave Mathias.)

In 1960, the Transmontane Company bought the Peter E. Kastos ranch, located about a mile and a half east of the Hanson Ranch. A Greek sheep rancher, Pete grazed sheep on both the front and back sides of No-Name Mountain. The sale of the Kastos Ranch was consummated at Pete's sheep camp, and the men sealed the deal with a shot of ouzo. (Courtesy of Sepp Cheny.)

Lionshead and the surrounding buildings took on a different look than the Bavarian-style Vail Village. It featured the clustered concrete look of some of the French resorts, such as Chamonix and Les Arcs. When Lionshead was completed, Vail boasted seven chairlifts, two gondolas, four beginner lifts, 28 restaurants, and a ski school with 70 instructors.

In the early days, people moved to Vail because they loved the environment, were crazy about skiing, and thirsted for adventure. Almost everyone in the lift lines knew everyone else. Five days after a powder storm, skiers could still cut fresh tracks in the back bowls. With Mount of the Holy Cross in the background, these skiers take a break at the top of Chair 4. (Courtesy of Barry Stott/Stott Shot.)

To launch the cars in the main gondola in the winter or the summer, a lift operator had to run down the ramp pushing the car, getting it up to speed with the cable. The faster the push was, the less of a jolt when the car met up with the cable. Eventually, the Vail Village gondola was replaced with the Vista Bahn Chairlift. (Courtesy of Barry Stott/Stott Shot.)

Shown here in 1968, Sepp Cheny busts fresh powder in the back bowls. Sepp was a familiar face on the mountain, teaching skiing for 30 seasons. When Vail opened, the skier capacity was 1,500. By late winter of 1964, capacity had been reached six times that much. Easter Sunday 1964 found 2,000 skiers on the mountain. (Courtesy of Sepp Cheny.)

For more than 20 years, Jebbi Brown taught kids how to ski—both locals and visitors alike. In the summertime, Jebbi switched to swimming lessons and taught at the Vail Village Inn. In this 1970s-era photograph, Jebbie stands guard in the background as her class of young skiers demonstrates a "perfect piece of pie" as they ski down a beginner slope. (Courtesy of Jebbie Brown.)

In January 1963 at Denver's Stapleton Airport, a car rental agent told her customer that there was no such place as Vail, Colorado. She produced a map and pointed to Avon and Minturn, but insisted there was no Vail. By the early 1970s, everyone knew where Vail was located. Newcomers came for a season and stayed for a lifetime.

By the early 1970s, the ski school had grown to over 70 instructors. Seen here, members of the Vail Ski School parade up Bridge Street. In front are, from left to right, John Donovan, Bob Gagne, Jerry Muth, Eric Windish, Ludwig Kurtz, and Hadley Gray. Instructors either taught classes or gave private lessons. (Courtesy of Barry Stott/Stott Shot.)

In the early days of ski instruction for kids, the flat terrain east of Golden Peak was the learning area. There was no Magic Carpet Ski Lift or helper to catch children at the bottom of the hill. Children had to be five years old to attend ski school. Once they mastered a side step, wedge, snowplow, and right and left turn, they graduated to the Mighty Mite, which was a steel rope tow with handles about 20 feet apart. Some children fell while on the Mighty Mite, but determination compelled them to hang on. After they mastered the Mighty Mite, they graduated to the Poma Lift, which was as difficult to master as the Mighty Mite. Still, many kids loved to learn to ski and still do. Today, learning is a little easier for them. Here, Shirley Welch works with young skiers in 1970.

Seven

THE BOOM YEARS

Vail was now officially a ski area and a town. The right people had come together to do the necessary jobs. Don Almond, Vail's mountain manager, hired William "Sarge" Brown to help him in 1965. Sarge revamped both the trail crew and ski patrol. Robert Parker had put Vail on the map with his marketing techniques. Parker, Brown, US Ski Team coach Bob Beattie, and Serge Lang organized the International Ski Team races in Vail, a forerunner to today's FIS World Cup races. Beginning in 1965, when the hotshot names in ski racing were Jimmie Heuga, Billy Kidd, and Buddy Werner, races were held every year. When the town was buzzing with racers, it was a magical time, and nothing was more exciting than to see Jean-Claude Killy scream down Pepi's Face.

With the country in good economic times, skiing had become a fashionable sport. Condominiums in Vail sprang up like weeds. Real estate prices soared. In 1969, the Lionshead area of the resort opened. During the 1970s, Vail became known as the Western White House for Pres. Gerald R. Ford, who enjoyed vacationing in Vail with his family. Soon, television networks flashed pictures of Vail's slopes across the nation. Vail continued to grow at a staggering pace, and for easier to travel to Vail, I-70 was built over Vail Pass.

In the early 1970s, the Vail Ski Patrol is all smiles because members know about the Tuck 'Em Inn, a hunting tent near Riva Glade hidden from view from tourists and management. It was outfitted with a brass bed, queen-size mattress, satin sheets, lantern, throw rugs, a battery-operated phonograph, and a keg of beer. It gave hanky-panky a new meaning. When the tent was finally discovered and ordered dismantled, getting the queen-size mattress down Riva Ridge proved more difficult than anticipated. During one summer, tourists would look up at the face of Riva and marvel at the last square patch of snow. Any ski patroller who overheard this just chuckled, knowing that the snow was actually a mattress. Although ski patrollers were known for their high jinks, they were also professionals, trained to save lives and kept the mountain safe. (Courtesy of Sandy Hinmon.)

In this photograph, almost all the same ski patrollers seen in the previous photograph met 30 years later for patrolman Dick Dickson's memorial service. Dick was a patrolman for many years and a friend to all. In memory of Dick, the patrolmen raised a beer and recalled times at the Tuck'Em Inn. The memories kept everyone smiling. (Courtesy of Don Johnson.)

Race day was a good day on Vail Mountain in the early 1970s. Despite marginal snow during its first few years of operation, Vail became famous in future years for favorable early- and late-season conditions. Pictured in 1973, an unidentified racer on course sends up a cloud of snow as he sets his edges in perfect conditions to make a turn.

Ski racing became interwoven with Vail's growth and success. From its first season, Vail hosted races, which in turn garnered more publicity than marketing dollars could produce. Race crews made sure that the racecourse remained in good condition. Here, salt is tossed on the course to harden the snow.

Bob Parker, Pete Seibert, and US Alpine coach Bob Beattie created a series of International Ski Team races, a forerunner of today's FIS World Cup races. Held in 1965, 1967, and 1968, the races gave Vail international attention. In this photograph of an opening ceremony in 1967, Father Tom Stone blesses the racers from all nations in a ceremony before the first race.

From Vail's opening to present day, some of the best après-ski entertainment was at the Los Amigos deck. From racers to skiers who could not hold an edge, the challenge of surviving Pepi's Face gave lasting memories for skiers and viewers. Ski racing was entwined with Vail's success. First was the US Alpine Ski Team training camp, next came the first Vail Cup, and then the International Ski Team races, held in 1965, 1967, and 1969, which attracted a huge amount of national and international press coverage. The success of early racing in Vail brought the World Alpine Ski Championships in 1989 and again in 1999. Here, an unidentified racer in the International Ski Team races launches through the final turn of a race. World Cup racing will return to Vail in 2015.

Realizing that a resort town could not survive solely on wintertime activities, in 1967 Pete Seibert ushered in the Vail Golf Course, a nine-hole course designed by Pres Maxwell. For several years, the Arnold Palmer Golf Academy operated in Vail and was a golf-training center for young adults. (Courtesy of Barry Stott/Stott Shot.)

The 18-hole golf course was opened in 1969, after Pete Seibert, Rod Slifer, and Dick Hauserman designed the second nine holes by hitting golf balls into the sagebrush. Ben Kruger was golf course superintendent for 25 years. Here, Jack Nicklaus (at left in the golf cart) checks his scorecard during a golf tournament. (Courtesy of Vail Resorts.)

Bob Barrett, President Ford's military aide during his White House years, put together the first Jerry Ford Invitational Golf Tournament along with John Purcell, Rod Slifer, and John Donovan. Invitees included Bob Hope, Telly Savalas, Dinah Shore, Clint Eastwood, and the Statler Brothers. The event ran for more than 20 years. Here is Bob Hope admiring a mishit. (Courtesy of Diana Donovan.)

As a huge promoter of Vail, President Ford supported the Eagle River Scholarship Fund, which was established in 1977 and continues today. Endowed by the Jerry Ford Golf Tournament, the focus of the fund is to provide students with an opportunity to acquire skills for life. In this photograph, President Ford (right) presents the first check to Rod Slifer (left) and John Donovan. (Courtesy of Diana Donovan.)

In the early 1970s, Vail held town bicycle races, which started in Lionshead and looped through Vail and back to Lionshead. In 1978, the Coors Classic came to town. The races packed spectators five-deep along the streets to watch the cyclists. This event continued for 10 summers. In 1994, Vail hosted the World Mountain Bike Championships, and in the summer of 2011, professional cycling returned to town.

Since the beginning, the lift crew has been an important part of the mountain. The crew was responsible for keeping the lifts running safely. Seen here is the lift crew from the 1973–1974 season, from left to right, Joe Clark, Bob Mcilveen, Ted Rycek, Bill Chaney, Bob Munson, and Fred Hodkins.

Ski instructor jobs lasted through the winter; but in the summer, they had to find other employment. It was always a long stretch between seasons. Pictured in the summer of 1974 in front of the Blue Cow, which stood at the eastern end of the parking lot, ski school members gathered to show what they "did in the summer." Tyrolean in nature, the Blue Cow served food with a German flair and with waitresses in dirndls. In the summers, instructors rode horses, bikes, or fire engines. They worked as accountants and carpenters, waiters and bartenders. Some people seen in this photograph are B.J. Smith, Phil Kirchbaum, Mike Tennent, Don Welch, John Donovan, John Kirshner, and Ludwig Kurz. (Courtesy of Sepp Cheny.)

In 1975, as Colorado's centennial and the nation's bicentennial anniversary approached, a group of Colorado ski pioneers decided it was time to open a ski museum to preserve and interpret the history of skiing (and later snowboarding). A committee was formed to establish a nonprofit ski museum. Those involved in the project were Dudley Abbott, Bob Parker, Lou Livingston, Todd Martin, John Dobson, and others. The US Forest Service, Vail Associates, Colorado Ski Country, and the Eagle County Historical Society joined the efforts to develop the Colorado Ski Museum, which opened in 1977. The museum's first executive director was Rev. Don Simonton, and Dudley Abbott was the first president. A home was found at the former Mountain Bell building at Vail Road and East Meadow Drive to house the museum.

Inside the Colorado Ski & Snowboard Museum, visitors find displays of everything from ski garments to old-style equipment including skis, bindings, and lace boots. One of the most extensive exhibits illustrates Camp Hale and the importance of the 10th Mountain Division ski troops. Continuous videos with footage of Camp Hale can be seen. An original Bell gondola is also on display.

The museum displays photographs and printed biographies of all of the Colorado Ski and Snowboard Hall of Fame inductees aling with some items belonging to members. In 1978, the first Hall of Fame induction banquet was held to honor Coloradoans who had contributed to the sport of skiing and snowboarding in Colorado. Since then, more than 100 people have been inducted into the Hall of Fame. The nominees must have contributed significantly to the snow sport industry in the state of Colorado.

After 15 years, the museum needed a new home, because the Town of Vail planned to tear down the building. The town then gave the museum space in the Vail Transportation Center in the heart of Vail Village. In addition, the museum has space in Golden, Colorado, to hold artifacts and a research library.

The days of the sheep ranchers were not over by the late 1960s and early 1970s. This photograph was taken north of Gore Creek somewhere in an open space above where Safeway is today. The sheepherder has his portable home stationed there. In the background, the Chamonix Chalets condominiums are visible. (Courtesy of Sandy Hinmon.)

Summertime continued to attract visitors. With the golf course completed, tennis courts in place, gold medal fishing in Gore Creek, rafting on the Colorado River, visits to Piney Lake, gondola rides, hiking, music venues, and warm days and cool nights, Vail had everything to offer visitors, including spectacular scenery. This photograph on the Vail Golf Course is an example of a perfect day in Vail.

Wintertime continues to delight skiers and snowboarders. The mountain offers everything a die-hard powder junkie could crave, from the Lionshead cruisers to the famous back bowls. By 1985, Vail had four high-speed detachable quad chairs, including the bubbled Vista Bahn, Mountain Top, Northwoods, and Game Creek lifts. Pictured here in the 1960s, Roger Staub (center) and unidentified friends drift through incomparable Vail powder. (Courtesy of Barry Stott/Stott Shot.)

Before the Vail Chapel was built, Catholics celebrated Sunday morning Mass at the Casino amidst lingering beer and cigarette fumes from Saturday night ski patrol parties. In the summer of 1967, Rev. Don Simonton was asked to develop an "experimental ministry" in Vail. He developed the interfaith concept, allowing different denominations to use the same worship area. A onetime park ranger, avid historian, and storyteller, Don was the perfect fit to host Vail's first chapel, built in 1969 on donated land from Vail Associates. Below the chapel was a beaver pond, which at one time—and when frozen—was the only ice rink in Vail. At nights, spirited games of broomball would take place. Today, six religious congregations share the Vail Chapel, and Don Simonton and his wife, June, are happily retired.

Eight

GROWTH AND CHANGES

Vail and Lionshead continued to rapidly grow. By the spring of 1976, five million skiers had skied Vail. The town of Vail grew as well. In 1977, Judge Buck Allen collected $5,729 in fines, and he collected $45,703 in 1981. The increase was attributed to police efficiency. Then, on a Friday morning in March 1976, Vail faced a crisis. Two of the Lionshead gondolas fell. Over 200 skiers in 39 gondola cars were stranded. Heroes were created everywhere that day, from the patrolmen who rescued those stranded in the cars to medical teams who treated injuries. Shortly thereafter, Vail Associates sold the company to board member Harry Bass. Harry fired Pete Seibert. However, Pete had left Harry a gem in the rough: Beaver Creek for future development.

In the 1970s and 1980s, Vail Village continued to thrive. It now had paved streets, 20,000 beds for guests, a golf course, an ice arena, and a library. In 1984, George Gillett, who had ties to the meatpacking and broadcasting industries, purchased Vail. George mingled with guests and employees and brought fun back to the resort. He installed high-speed chairlifts and opened China Bowl. During George's tenure, Vail was named the number one ski resort in North America by *Skiing* and *Ski* magazines. In the late 1980s, the Gerald R. Ford Amphitheater opened, and in 1987, the hospital completed a major expansion. When the Gillett Group became overextended, Apollo Partners bought the company out of bankruptcy. Apollo then acquired Keystone and Breckenridge from Ralston Purina. With four ski areas, Vail Resorts became the largest single ski area operator in Colorado's ski industry.

George Gillett (pictured) and Pete Seibert had similar passions—the mountain, people, and skiing. George shook hands with employees. He smiled a lot. He loved to ski. He opened China Bowl and brought international attention to Vail by staging the 1989 World Alpine Championships. It was a fun time to work and ski in Vail.

In the 1960s, Chupa Nelson came to Vail and joined the ski patrol. In this photograph taken behind Sandstone Condominiums west of Sandstone Creek, Chupa looks unsure of himself riding his horse Headlight. That day in March 1976 when the gondolas fell, Chupa did not display any fear as he skimmed along the damaged cable, 100 feet above the ground, to chain damaged gondola cars to the cable. (Courtesy of Sandy Hinmon.)

Just as skiing was taking off in Vail, along came something designed more like a surfboard with comfortable boots. It was called a snowboard, and it was first introduced to Vail Mountain during the 1987–1988 season during a two-month trial period. Many young skiers who had become complacent with skis found the new equipment challenging and exciting. That year, there were about 200,000 snowboarders nationwide.

The next season, snowboarders were welcomed year-round to the mountain. Although Larry Litchlighter, executive vice president of mountain operations, assumed it would grow, Vail had no plans to build a half-pipe or terrain park. Today, snowboarders account for more than six million riders nationwide. It is an Olympic sport, and riders can get "big air." (Photograph by Jack Afleck.)

In the 1980s and early 1990s, Vail held Bartender's Races, which gave the workers a chance to have fun. Bartenders, barkeepers, barmaids, waiters, waitresses, hosts, dishwashers, doormen, prep cooks, solo guitar players, and band members all turned out for a day on the racecourse. Hardly any locals won the race, however, because most businesses had racers on their staff.

China Bowl opened to the public on December 3, 1988. The expansion also included Tea Cup, Siberia, and Mongolia Bowls. The added terrain—1,881 acres—made Vail the biggest ski resort in the country. China Bowl was named because the cliffs near the top of the Orient Express Lift reminded Vail founder Peter Seibert of the Great Wall of China.

Vail offers public and private schools, and Ski Club Vail has special school programs for its skiers. The Vail public high school, Battle Mountain, was located in Eagle-Vail. In this 1993 photograph, the high school's production of the musical *Grease* is in full swing. In the first decade of the 21st century, the high school became too small, and a new campus was built in Edwards.

In the predawn hours of October 19, 1998, commando-style arsonists destroyed $12 million worth of chairlifts and Two Elk Lodge at the top of China Bowl, shown here overlooking the bowl. The Earth Liberation Front claimed responsibility, saying it felt that lynx were threatened by the expansion of Vail into Blue Sky Basin.

Bill Wright's 1990 Summer Tennis Camp Vail, Colorado

For 27 years, Bill Wright was the director of tennis at the Gold Peak and Ford Park tennis courts. After coaching at the University of California and 19 years at the University of Arizona, Bill was inducted into the Intercollegiate Tennis Association Hall of Fame in 2006. Every child in Vail attended his summer tennis camps. This is his group in 1992. (Courtesy of Vail Tennis Center.)

An anonymous donation of $300,000 helped build Dobson Ice Arena in 1978 and 1979. Named for Vail's mayor John Dobson, the 35,000-square-foot facility hosts concerts, ice hockey games, ice skating competitions, and special events. The Bob Johnson Ice Hockey School has been held at Dobson for more than 25 summers.

Vail has boasted a strong junior hockey program since the early days. First, hockey players practiced on the ice rink at the golf course and then relocated to Dobson after the arena was built. Merv Lapin, a town councilman and former mayor, has taken high school hockey players to China and Russia to enhance their cultural awareness. This is a photograph of the high school hockey team in 1992.

Vail medical facilities began as a clinic adjacent to the kitchen of the Red Lion and then moved to the Plaza Building, which had two exam rooms, an X-ray room, and a waiting room. When the clinic moved to its present location, the facility had accommodations for four patients. Today, the hospital provides comprehensive medical care with over 190 physicians, 58 acute beds, and professional and support staff of over 700.

In the early 1980s, hang gliding became a new fad. Those crazy enough to try it decided it would be a great addition to skiing. Enter the ski patrol boys. They began testing hang gliding on short gliders, but found that did not work. They moved up to bigger kites and still found trouble launching them. Getting out their speed guns, the patrol boys found that liftoff could be accomplished at 30 miles per hour, so someone stayed on the ground with the gun and gave the thumbs up when 30 mile per hour had been reached. In this photograph, Sandy Hinmon completes a final sweep over the back bowls with a dramatic view of the Sawatch Range behind him. It is not known what would have happened if Sandy spotted a lost skier, nor is it known how he made it back to patrol headquarters that day. Hang gliding came to a rapid end before gaining solid footing on Vail Mountain. (Courtesy of Sandy Hinmon.)

Nine

LIKE NOTHING ON EARTH

When Vail entered the new millennium, the 40-year-old resort needed renovations. The gondola and terminal in Lionshead were dismantled to make way for the upscale Arabelle development. The old Crossroads in Vail Village disappeared to be replaced by Solaris. The Four Seasons came to town, as did the Ritz-Carlton Residences. For several years, it seemed as though construction sites were as visible as panoramic views. On the mountain during the 2010–2011 season, the infamous Chair 5 in the back bowls was replaced by a high-speed quad lift, and the Epic Pass holders could see how many vertical feet they had skied each day. The winter of 2011 turned epic, resulting in the most snowfall on record.

What next? Enter Ever Vail. Located west of Lionshead, Ever Vail will be Vail's next development. As a resort of the future, it will feature a gondola, parking, residential units, and a new hotel and conference space. After 50 years of growth, Vail Resorts and the Town of Vail have realized what works and what does not. When Ever Vail is complete, it will be a showcase as North America's largest green-built resort. Vail Village, Lionshead,. Ever Vail—the story just gets bigger and better. From the moment Pete Seibert and Earl Eaton first hiked up No-Name Mountain until today, Vail has become the greatest ski area ever built. What an accomplishment! Happy Birthday, Vail!

The Mount of the Holy Cross is seen in this photograph from Bells Camp in Blue Sky Basin. In the 1920s, people came from all over the country in the summer to make a pilgrimage to the cross with the belief in spiritual healing. In this photograph, former patrolman Dave Stanish and his wife, Kasey, pause to take in the view.

Donovan Park and Pavilion was dedicated to John F. Donovan for his years of service on Vail Town Council and other town boards. It is also dedicated to John for the softball games, the cleanup days, the "raise," the planting of trees, the storytelling, the Fourth of July parade, the golf tournaments, Ducks Unlimited, and on and on.

In the early days, the Town of Vail Master Plan determined that the property where Crossroads was to be built was only good for a dog kennel or Laundromat. Up sprang Crossroads, which remained until the mid-2000s. Next came Solaris, built to create effortless mountain living. It has an upscale movie theater and a 10-lane bowling alley.

Ever Vail will be built just to the right of Simba ski trail, seen in this photograph. A gondola will go from the village on the valley floor to the top of the mountain. The expanse of Vail will continue. Many visitors can see the front side of Vail Mountain and how big it is, but they cannot see the expanse of the massive back bowls.

The Fourth of July parade is a Vail tradition. From children on bikes to the Lawn Chair Demonstration Team to Irish dancers, horses, bands, and magicians, the parade never fails to thrill viewers. In 2011, close to 30,000 people watched the parade under cloudless skies.

The Fourth of July parade would not be complete without Jerry Sibley and his vintage steam engine, as shown in this photograph. Besides teaching skiing, Jerry established a plumbing company in Vail's early years; it still serves the Vail Valley. Below his shop in Minturn, Jerry restores vintage cars and motorcycles.

In 1987, the Bravo! Vail Valley Music Festival was created by attorney John Giovando and acclaimed violinist Ida Kavafian. What started as a small festival now draws more than 60,000 attendees. The Philadelphia Orchestra plays Broadway music at the Ford Amphitheater in this photograph.

Currently in its 25th year, the Bravo! Festival runs from late June through early August, presenting the highest level of music in spectacular Vail Valley venues. The festival touches the lives of thousands of people, many who come to the area specifically to experience the pleasures of musical performances and the beauty of the Rocky Mountains.

In the summer of 2011, the first Wings and Wheels car show took place. First was a display at the airport in Gypsum, which included vintage cars, airplanes, and helicopters. Next, the show moved to Vail Village, where vintage cars were displayed throughout town. Visitors could view the cars and chat with the owners.

Since the first settlers came to the Gore Creek Valley, fishing in Gore Creek has been nothing less than spectacular. The gold medal section starts at Red Sandstone Creek and continues west to the Eagle River. The limit is two fish and is catch and release. Patrick Welch shows his catch of the day in 2001.

Vail continues to thrill skiers and snowboarders. From the front side of the mountain to the endless back bowls to Pete Seibert and Earl Eaton's Bowls in Blue Sky Basin, the delights of a day on the mountain seem endless: hot chocolate at Two Elk Lodge, big air off the cliffs in Blue Sky Basin, ski races, and powder days.

Willy Schaeffler wrote in a 1960s *Sports Illustrated* article that Vail would never be successful because it did not have enough steep terrain. That article started a flood of phone reservations when people learned the entire family could ski Vail. Bill and Mary Flanagan from Pennsylvania have vacationed in Vail for more than 35 years. Here, they ride Chair 14, headed for China Bowl.

Although Larry Litchlighter, a former Vail executive and industry icon, would not agree that terrain parks for snowboarders were necessary, they have become state-of-the-art on Vail Mountain. Snowboarders young and old can test their skills, balance, and big air jumps on any number of terrain parks. This is on Golden Peak in the winter of 2011.

The charm of Vail Village has remained constant for nearly 50 years. With the backdrop of the Gore Range to the east of the village and mountain, the awe-inspiring pinnacles of the peaks continue to enchant and delight through every season. Even during Vail's renaissance, the Gore Range remained a constant in the life of the village. (Courtesy of Barry Stott, Stott Shot.)

Olympic Gold Medal champion Lindsey Vonn began skiing at age three. From Minnesota, her family moved to Vail when she was 12. She competed in her first Olympics at age 17 and is the most successful female skier in America. In February 2010, Vail's International Ski Run was renamed Lindsey's. This is a display board of Lindsey at the Colorado Ski & Snowboard Museum.

Vail's most famous landmark, the Covered Bridge, remains as quaint as it did in the early 1960s when the Dobsons funded half of the construction costs to cover the bridge over Gore Creek, thus ensuring that their building name along the creek had merit. Today, hundreds of thousands of skiers cross the bridge to reach the base of the lifts for an epic day of skiing.

Gore Creek Drive still exudes the quaint Bavarian feeling that has charmed visitors and residents alike for more than 50 years. A stroll down Gore Creek Drive from west to east highlights the dramatic panorama of the Gore Range. Walking from east to west presents a visual display of architecture from the Children's Fountain to the shuttered buildings.

As the decades passed, new and upscale properties were built. Nestled at the base of Vail Mountain, The Ritz-Carlton Residences is one of them. Jutting out of a forest of pine, it is reminiscent of a castle. Located at the west end of Lionshead, the Ritz-Carlton will be at the eastern end of the new Ever Vail development. (Courtesy of Vail Resorts.)

Another upscale development was built at the base of Vail Mountain along the hillside adjacent to Lindsey's run. Vail Chalets give owners some of the best ski-in and ski-out property in Vail. In the afternoon, those in residence have a bird's-eye view of Pepi's Face and those brave souls who make the attempt to ski it. (Courtesy of Vail Resorts.)

From the beginning, what Vail had that was incomparable was an abundance of light snow, wide-open bowl skiing, terrain for every ability, and a feeling that made every visitor important. The same criteria are in place today. The snow is great; the sky is blue; the ambiance, epic. There is no place like it on earth.

Just when Vail's renaissance was complete and no one thought it could get much better, along came Ever Vail. The proposed Ever Vail project has been in the Town of Vail approval process since 2007. The $1 billion project, anticipated to open in a few years, will transform a 9.5-acre site currently known as West Lionshead into a sustainable, multiuse pedestrian village. The village will consist of residences, a hotel, offices, retail shops, restaurants, mountain operations facilities, a public parking garage, a new gondola and related skier portal, and a public park. This development is one of the first projects to be accepted into the US Green Building Council's new Leadership in Energy and Environmental Design for Neighborhood Development (LEED-ND) certification program. (Courtesy of Vail Resorts.)

Pete Seibert

1924 — 2002

Vail, CO

Pete Seibert and Earl Eaton are gone, but what they created will forever be a reminder of their dream. From the time Pete was a child, he was magic on skis. Although he suffered injuries more severe than most people could endure, he found a way to ski again, and he skied with passion and grace. Earl pursued his goals, making dreams come true for the first generation of Vail residents and continuing even today. Vail is full of first-, second-, and third-generation residents. It is also the playground for ski enthusiasts from all over the nation and the world. What a dream! An ending poem on the back of Pete's memorial program includes a quote from his book *Vail, Triumph of Dream* that was adapted from text in T.E. Lawrence's *Seven Pillars of Wisdom*: "Those who dream by night in the dusty recesses of their minds wake in the morning to find that all was vanity; but the dreamers of the day are dangerous . . . for they may act on their dream . . . and make it possible." Thank you, Pete and Earl, for making Vail possible.

Visit us at
arcadiapublishing.com

Ingram Content Group UK Ltd.
Milton Keynes UK
UKHW032147180423
420401UK00010B/191